KIDS ASK™

How?

Illustrations by Marilee Harrald-Pilz

Publications International, Ltd.

How does a television work?

ActiveMinds is a registered trademark of Publications International, Ltd.
Kids Ask is a trademark of Publications International, Ltd.

Louis Weber, CEO
Publications International, Ltd.
7373 North Cicero Avenue
Lincolnwood, Illinois 60712

www.myactiveminds.com

Permission is never granted for commercial purposes.

ISBN-13: 978-1-4127-1239-2
ISBN-10: 1-4127-1239-4

Manufactured in China.

8 7 6 5 4 3 2 1

Contents

How do elephants use their trunks?

How do fish breathe underwater?

Fish use their gills to get oxygen from the water. People do not have gills, so we cannot breathe underwater, and fish do not have lungs, so they cannot breathe outside of water.

FUN FACT

Whales and dolphins might look like fish, but they are *mammals* like us. They have lungs, and they have to go to the surface to breathe.

How deep is the ocean?

The ocean is really shallow near shore—it barely covers your toes! But there are some places, called trenches, where the ocean may be seven miles deep. Even the highest mountain on land is not that high! The water down there is very cold and very dark.

How big were dinosaurs?

Dinosaurs came in all sizes. The smallest dinosaur was the size of a chicken. Other dinosaurs were bigger than a school bus. *Brachiosaurus* was one of the largest dinosaurs—it was over 80 feet long and weighed as much as 10 elephants!

How long ago did dinosaurs live?

Dinosaurs lived a *really* long time ago. The first dinosaurs lived over 230 million years ago. The last dinosaurs died about 65 million years ago, a long time before humans showed up.

FUN FACT

You might think dinosaur eggs would be huge, but the biggest ones were only about the size of a volleyball.

How did people tell time before there were clocks?

People have been telling time for thousands of years. At first people used the sun to help them. They measured how long shadows were to tell what time of day it was. Later, people made sundials that measured shadows as they moved around a dial like a watch hand.

FUN FACT

Before watches and clocks were invented, people also measured the sand flowing through an hourglass to tell time.

990

9

How does an airplane fly?

An airplane is heavier than air. It can fly because its wings are a special shape—they have a flat bottom, a round front, and a curved top. The wings direct the air so that it lifts the plane. The faster the plane goes, the greater the lift. That is why a plane must go really fast down a runway to take off.

FUN FACT

A sheep, a duck, and a chicken were the first creatures to fly in a hot air balloon!

How do people steer a hot air balloon?

The only directions a balloonist can control are up and down. Going forward or backward depends on the wind. People who travel in balloons must know a lot about the wind. They must know how high and how fast different layers of wind, called *currents,* blow.

How do horses sleep?

Horses usually sleep standing up. Their legs lock in place to keep the animal from falling over. Horses can lie down, but because they are heavy, it takes a lot of energy for them to get back up. You should not try to sleep standing up—your knees do not lock, and you will probably fall over!

FUN FACT

A baby horse learns to walk only an hour or two after being born.

How do Inuits
stay warm in an igloo?

Inuits live in a very cold climate. They light fires inside their igloos to keep warm. They also cut holes in the top of the igloo for the smoke to escape. The air outside is so cold that even with a fire burning inside the walls do not melt.

How many animals live in the Arctic?

The Arctic is one of the coldest spots on Earth. But plenty of animals are built for surviving in such a harsh place. Caribou, mice, seals, snowy owls, foxes, and polar bears are just some of the animals that live in the snow and ice.

FUN FACT

A polar bear's nose is so sensitive it can smell a seal on the ice 20 miles away!

How does a telephone work?

When you talk into a telephone, your voice makes wires in the phone vibrate. The telephone changes these vibrations into *energy*. This energy can travel anywhere in the world. When the energy reaches another phone, it is changed back into sound. The person listening hears you loud and clear, even if you are miles away!

How does a television work?

Have you ever seen a flip-book, where a character looks like it is moving when you flip the pages really fast? A TV works the same way, only faster. TV cameras take lots and lots of pictures. Thirty pictures are sent to your TV every second! These pictures are shown so quickly that the images on the screen look like they are moving.

How high can a kangaroo jump?

A kangaroo has powerful hind legs and a strong tail that helps it balance. Using its legs and tail, a kangaroo can jump up to 10 feet high—as high as a basketball hoop. And when it is hopping as fast as it can, a kangaroo can also jump as far as 40 feet in one leap!

FUN FACT

A baby kangaroo will stay in its mother's pouch until it is more than a year old.

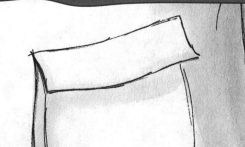

How does a broken bone heal?

As soon as a bone is broken it begins to heal. The brain sends messages to the bone to tell it to start growing back together. Most people need to wear a cast or a splint to keep the bone in the right position, because it takes a while for the bone to heal.

How does an X-ray machine work?

X-rays are like light, but they can pass through more materials than light. Light cannot pass through your body, but an X-ray can. Bones block X-rays more than other things in your body do, so when an X-ray machine takes a picture of your body, your bones show up very well. A doctor looks at the X-ray picture to see if anything is wrong with your bones.

How can a camel live in the desert?

The desert is really dry, so when a camel finds water it will drink up to 20 gallons at one time. That way, it can go a really long time without having to drink again. A camel also has wide, thick feet that do not sink in the sand and are not hurt by heat, stones, or thorns.

How does a snake move without legs?

A s-s-s-nake has a long backbone made of many smaller bones and ribs. When the snake moves, its muscles bend and move this long line of bones. Some snakes can move in a straight line. Others use their bodies to s-s-s-lither along the ground in curves.

FUN FACT

The spitting cobra can shoot venom out of its teeth up to eight feet away!

How does a sea otter eat?

A sea otter likes to eat fish that live in shells, but the shells can be really hard to open. An otter holds a shell on its stomach as it floats in the water on its back. Then it hits the shell with a rock to break it open. Inside is the tasty treat! The otter uses its stomach as a dinner table, too.

FUN FACT

A sea otter eats almost 5,000 pounds of food a year!

5,000 LBS.

How big is the moon?

The moon is one-fourth as big as the earth. Even though the moon looks bigger than any of the stars, it is not. It only appears that way because it is so much closer to the earth than the stars are.

FUN FACT

There is no wind or weather on the moon. The footprints left by astronauts will be there forever.

How many stars are in the sky?

If you tried to count the stars on a very clear night, far from the lights of cities and towns, you might count about 3,000. With the help of a powerful telescope you could count a lot more. There are millions and millions of stars in the universe.

Fun Fact

Some roller coasters go over 120 miles per hour. That is almost twice as fast as a car on the highway!

121 MPH

How does a roller coaster stay on the track?

Roller coasters are held on the track by three sets of wheels. There is one set of wheels on top of the track, similar to the tires on a car. There are also wheels on the side of the track and even on the bottom of the track. All these wheels lock the roller coaster to the track—a roller coaster can even do loops and go upside down without falling off!

How do elephants use their trunks?

Elephants use their trunks to smell and to push and pull. They pick up food and other small things with the two fingerlike parts at the end of their trunks. They can also warn other elephants of danger by trumpeting through their trunks. Elephants even give themselves baths with their trunks by sucking up water and spraying it over their heads.

How fast can a cheetah run?

The cheetah is the fastest land animal on Earth. A cheetah has strong legs and a long tail that helps it balance as it runs. Its claws are always out, and they help the cheetah get a good grip on the ground. A cheetah is built for speed, and it can run up to 70 miles an hour! But that is tiring work, so a cheetah can only run that fast for a short time.

How much can people learn?

The brain is an amazing thing. Even though it is not very large, the brain can store enormous amounts of information. People can learn just about anything they want to learn. Scientists say that people do not even use their entire brain. Imagine how much more you could learn if you used your whole brain!